And Everyone Shouted, "Pull!"
A First Look at Forces and Motion

by Claire Llewellyn   illustrated by Simone Abel

Special thanks to our reading adviser:

Susan Kesselring, M.A., Literacy Educator
Rosemount-Apple Valley-Eagan (Minnesota) School District

PICTURE WINDOW BOOKS
Minneapolis, Minnesota

First American edition published in 2005 by
Picture Window Books
5115 Excelsior Boulevard
Suite 232
Minneapolis, MN 55416
877-845-8392
www.picturewindowbooks.com

First published in Great Britain in 2002 by Hodder Wayland,
Hodder Children's Books
A division of Hodder Headline Limited
338 Euston Road
London NW1 3BH

Printed in the United States of America.

Library of Congress Cataloging-in-Publication Data
Llewellyn, Claire.
And everyone shouted, "Pull!" : a first look at forces and motion
/ by Claire Llewellyn ; illustrated by Simone Abel.
p. cm.—(First look : science)
ISBN 1-4048-0656-3
1. Force and energy—Juvenile literature. 2. Motion—Juvenile
literature. I. Abel, Simone, ill. II. Title. III. Series.
QC73.4.L45 2005
531'.6—dc22   2004007310

For Helena, Dominic, and Gabriella – C.L.
For John Hodgson, with love – S.A.

the animals are counting out the goods.

... and don't forget the cheese.

5

Its wheels help move things easily.

I wish I had wheels!

9

The cart's wheels can't move by themselves.

10

The first few steps are hard work ...

12

but then the wheels begin to turn.

The cart rolls along quickly now.

Keep up!

But when the cart reaches Three Trees Hill,

Push, everyone!

17

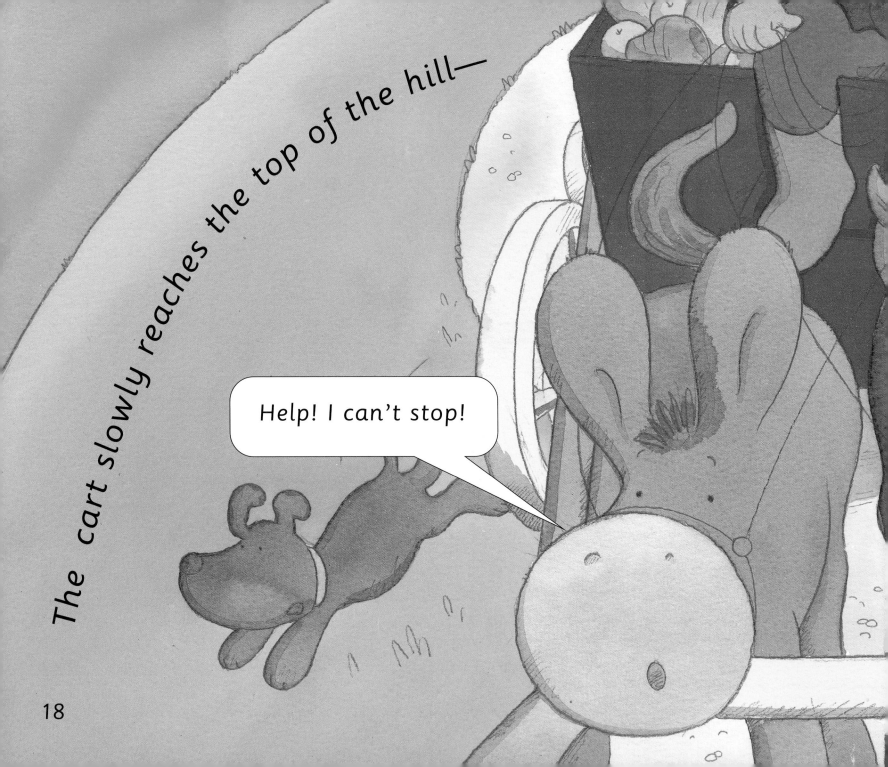

The cart slowly reaches the top of the hill—

18

19

The cart is pulled another way.

21

We're not moving, Mama!

Big drops of rain begin to fall.

22

The ground turns soft and muddy.

23

At last, the cart arrives at the market.

25

The market is over. It's time to go home.

But the cart isn't empty, after all.

All About Forces

Moving a load is hard work. Wheels make it easier to move things.

PUSH

PULL

It takes a force to start things moving.

A force can be a pull or a push.

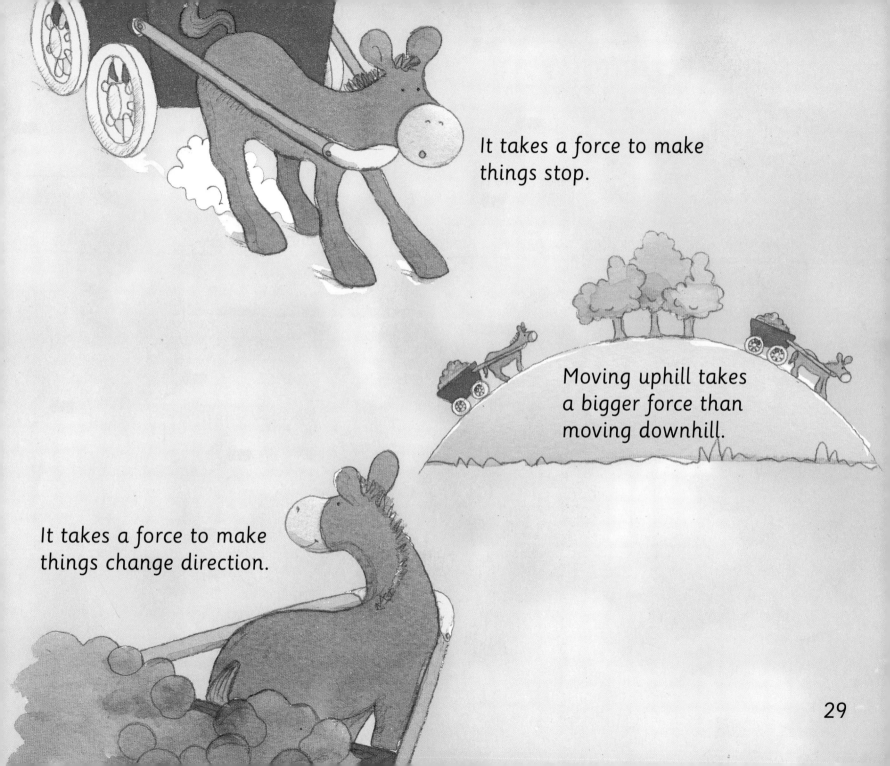

It takes a force to make things stop.

Moving uphill takes a bigger force than moving downhill.

It takes a force to make things change direction.

29

Useful Words

Downhill
Down a slope.

Force
A push or a pull that
makes an object start
moving, go faster,
change direction, slow
down, or stop.

Pull
To tug something.

Push
To move something forward
in front of you.

Uphill
Up a slope.

Fun Facts

 Sir Isaac Newton discovered three laws of motion that explain the way objects move.

 Nobody knows who invented the first wheel.

 Wheels were put on carts in 3500 b.c. This was the first wheeled vehicle in history.

 The oldest wheel ever found is about 5,500 years old.

To Learn More

At the Library

Challoner, Jack. *Push and Pull.* Austin, Tex.: Raintree-Steck Vaughn, 1997.

Cooper, Christopher. *Forces and Motion: From Push to Shove.* Chicago: Heinemann Library, 2003.

Stille, Darlene R. *Motion: Push and Pull, Fast and Slow.* Minneapolis: Picture Window Books, 2004.

On the Web

FactHound offers a safe, fun way to find Web sites related to this book. All of the sites on FactHound have been researched by our staff. *www.facthound.com*

1. Visit the FactHound home page.
2. Enter a search word related to this book, or type in this special code: 1404806563.
3. Click the FETCH IT button.

Your trusty FactHound will fetch the best Web sites for you!

Index

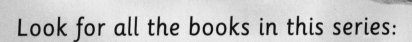

Look for all the books in this series:

A Seed in Need
A First Look at the Plant Cycle

Paint a Sun in the Sky
A First Look at the Seasons

The Drop Goes Plop
A First Look at the Water Cycle

And Everyone Shouted, "Pull!"
A First Look at Forces of Motion

Take a Walk on a Rainbow
A First Look at Color

The Hen Can't Help It
A First Look at the Life Cycle of a Chicken

From Little Acorns ...
A First Look at the Life Cycle of a Tree

The Case of the Missing Caterpillar
A First Look at the Life Cycle of a Butterfly

The Trouble with Tadpoles
A First Look at the Life Cycle of a Frog